THE BILL OF RIGHTS

Congress of the United States,
begun and held at the City of New-York, on
Wednesday the fourth of March, one thousand seven hundred and eighty-nine.

THE

RESOLVED

BY SETH LYNCH

Gareth Stevens
PUBLISHING

CRASH COURSE

Please visit our website, www.garethstevens.com. For a free color catalog of all our high-quality books, call toll free 1-800-542-2595 or fax 1-877-542-2596.

Library of Congress Cataloging-in-Publication Data

Names: Lynch, Seth.
Title: The Bill of Rights / Seth Lynch.
Description: New York : Gareth Stevens Publishing, 2019. | Series: A look at US history | Includes index.
Identifiers: LCCN ISBN 9781538221174 (pbk.) | ISBN 9781538221150 (library bound) | ISBN 9781538221181 (6 pack)
Subjects: LCSH: United States. Constitution. 1st-10th Amendments--Juvenile literature. | Civil rights--United States--History--Juvenile literature. | Constitutional history--United States--Juvenile literature.
Classification: LCC KF4749.L96 2019 | DDC 342.7308'5--dc23

First Edition

Published in 2019 by
Gareth Stevens Publishing
111 East 14th Street, Suite 349
New York, NY 10003

Copyright © 2019 Gareth Stevens Publishing

Designer: Samantha DeMartin
Editor: Kristen Nelson

Photo credits: Series art Christophe BOISSON/Shutterstock.com; (feather quill) Galushko Sergey/Shutterstock.com; (parchment) mollicart-design/Shutterstock.com; cover, p. 1 (photo) MarshalN20/Wikimedia Commons; cover, p. 1 (article) Larrybob/Wikimedia Commons; p. 5 SuperStock/SuperStock/Getty Images; p. 7 Jack R Perry Photography/Shutterstock.com; p. 9 (inset) Bettmann/Bettmann/Getty Images; p. 9 (main) Everett Historical/Shutterstock.com; p. 11 Illerlok_Xolms/Shutterstock.com; p. 13 NYCStock/Shutterstock.com; p. 15 Sony Herdiana/Shutterstock.com; p. 17 JEWEL SAMAD/AFP/Getty Images; p. 19 wavebreakmedia/Shutterstock.com; p. 21 Guy Call/Corbis/Getty Images; p. 23 sirtravelalot/Shutterstock.com; p. 25 Pacific Press/LightRocket/Getty Images; p. 27 Bloomberg/Bloomberg/Getty Images.

Printed in the United States of America

CPSIA compliance information: Batch #CS18GS: For further information contact Gareth Stevens, New York, New York at 1-800-542-2595.

CONTENTS

Words in the glossary appear in **bold** type the first time they are used in the text.

A NEW CONSTITUTION

By 1787, it was clear the **Articles of Confederation** had many problems. **Representatives** from 12 US states met to try to fix the Articles. They realized they needed a new **constitution**. However, some wouldn't **ratify** it unless it had a list of citizens' rights.

Those in favor of ratifying the Constitution as it was written were called Federalists. Anti-Federalists didn't support the Constitution as it was written.

The Anti-Federalists worried the **federal** government would be too powerful without a list of rights. They wanted to **protect** states' and citizens' rights. Finally, enough leaders agreed, and it was decided a Bill of Rights would be added. The Constitution was ratified in 1788.

MAKE THE GRADE

James Madison was a Federalist in support of the Constitution. But later, he was in favor of including a Bill of Rights in the **document**.

7

WRITING THE RIGHTS

Madison began working on the Bill of Rights by trying to change the US Constitution. He presented his ideas to Congress on June 8, 1789. However, it was decided the Bill of Rights would be a separate part of the Constitution.

MAKE THE GRADE

The Virginia Declaration of Rights, written by George Mason in 1776, was one document Madison looked to as he wrote the Bill of Rights.

James Madison

(Copy of the first Draught by G Ma.)

A Declaration of Rights made by the Representatives of the good People of Virginia assembled in full and free Convention; wh Rights do pertain to them and their posteri as the Basis and Foundation of Governm

1. That all men are created equally free & independent, & certain inherent natural Rights, of which they can not, any Compact deprive or divest their posterity; amongst are the Enjoyment of Life & Liberty, with the Means of acquiring possessing Property & pursuing & obtaining Happiness & Safety.

2. That all Power is by God & Nature vested in, & conseque derived from the people; that Magistrates are their Truste Servants, and at all Times amenable to them.

3. That Government is or ought to be instituted for the common Benefit, protection & Security of the People, Na or Community. Of all the various modes & Forms of Gove ment that is best, which is capable of producing the greate Degree of Happiness & Safety, & is most effectually secured aga the Danger of mal administration; and that whenever any G vernment shall be found inadequate or contrary to these p poses a majority of the Community hath an indubitable una able irenfeasible Right, to reform, alter, or abolish it. such

274 Page from a copy of the first draft of the Bill of Rights, from the original in the Virginia State Library, Richmond

SENT TO THE STATES

The US House of Representatives approved a list of 17 **amendments**. The Senate approved 12 of those amendments on September 25, 1789. These were sent to the states. Each amendment needed three-fourths of the states to ratify it to become part of the Constitution.

MAKE THE GRADE

The Constitution can also be amended when two-thirds of the states call for a Constitutional Convention. The amendments they present still need to be ratified by three-fourths of the states. This has never been done.

The United States, 1790

MA

NH

MA

RI

NY

CT

PA

NJ

DE

VA

NC

SC

GA

US TERRITORIES OR CLAIMED AREAS

FOREIGN AREAS

11

THE AMENDMENTS

Only 10 of the 12 possible amendments were ratified by the states. These make up the Bill of Rights. The First Amendment is one of the most important today. It states that citizens have freedom of speech and freedom of the press.

MAKE THE GRADE

The First Amendment also says citizens have the right to assemble peacefully, such as in **protest** of a law or government action.

WE ARE HERE TO **PROTECT**

WATER IS SACRED

The First Amendment also **guarantees** freedom of religion. This means citizens can believe and practice whatever faith they want. This was an important right to include as many people had come to the American colonies looking for religious freedom.

MAKE THE GRADE

The last right guaranteed under the First Amendment is the freedom to petition, or ask the government to address things it may have done wrong.

THE SECOND AMENDMENT

When the Bill of Rights was written, it was important for the states to have a strong **militia**. The Second Amendment states that citizens have the right to "keep and bear arms." Today, this usually means guns, but back then it may have meant swords, too!

MAKE THE GRADE

According to the Third Amendment, citizens can't be forced
to quarter, or keep, soldiers in their homes.

ALL RIGHTS come
to the PEOPLE
DIRECTLY from
the CREATOR
The SECOND
AMENDMENT is
MY RIGHT - NOT
e CITY'S, STATE'S,
or FEDERAL
OVERNMENT'S

SELF -
DEFENSE

IS A

BASIC
HUMAN
RIGHT!

2ND AMENDMENT
IT's NOT A "PRIVILEGE"
IT's MY RIGHT !

FOR THOSE ACCUSED

The Fourth Amendment states that the government can't search or take a person's belongings without a **warrant**. The Fifth Amendment has a number of rights outlined in it. One is that if the government takes a person's property, the person is paid for it.

MAKE THE GRADE

The Fourth and Fifth Amendments have to do with protecting the rights of people who have been **accused** of breaking the law.

Another right found in the Fifth Amendment protects "due process of law." This means that a set of laws must be followed when someone is accused of a crime. The laws make sure the person is tried fairly.

MAKE THE GRADE

Under the Sixth Amendment, people accused of crimes are guaranteed a "speedy and public" trial.

In the Seventh Amendment, it's stated that any civil, or noncriminal, cases are tried by a **jury** if the property in question is worth more than $20. In the Eighth Amendment, citizens are protected against "cruel and unusual punishment."

MAKE THE GRADE

The Eighth Amendment also states that people shouldn't have to pay very large fines or bail. Bail is the money people pay to be freed from jail before their trial.

MORE RIGHTS

The Ninth Amendment is less clear than the others. It states that citizens have rights not included in the Bill of Rights! It's meant to stop the federal government from increasing its power as well as protect other citizens' rights.

MAKE THE GRADE

There's no record of what other rights James Madison might have thought needed protection!

STATES' RIGHTS

The final part of the Bill of Rights, the Tenth Amendment, is another broad statement. It says that the states and those who live in the states are given any powers the Constitution doesn't give to the federal government.

The Constitution gives some very clear powers to Congress, the president, and the Supreme Court.

AMENDMENTS TODAY

The US Constitution is the oldest governing document still in use. Since the Bill of Rights was approved, 17 other amendments have been added. These changes make the Constitution's meaning clearer, make sure important rights are upheld, and make changes to how the government is run.

MAKE THE GRADE

The amendment process is long and often fails. Thousands of amendments have been proposed and not passed by Congress!

FAMOUS CONSTITUTIONAL AMENDMENTS

13TH AMENDMENT — ended slavery in the United States

14TH AMENDMENT — granted citizenship to everyone born in the United States, including former slaves freed by the Thirteenth Amendment

19TH AMENDMENT — gave women the right to vote

22ND AMENDMENT — limited the number of terms a president can serve to two

29

TIMELINE OF THE BILL OF RIGHTS

March 1, 1781

The first constitution of the United States, the Articles of Confederation, is ratified by the states.

September 3, 1783

The Treaty of Paris is signed, ending the American Revolution.

May 25, 1787

The Constitutional Convention, which writes a new US constitution, begins.

June 21, 1788

Three-fourths of the states ratify the Constitution, making it the highest law in the land.

June 8, 1789

Madison presents changes to the Constitution to Congress.

September 25, 1789

The Bill of Rights is presented to the states as a set of 12 amendments.

December 15, 1791

The Bill of Rights is ratified as 10 amendments.

GLOSSARY

accuse: to blame

amendment: a change or addition to a constitution

Articles of Confederation: the first US constitution, in effect from 1777 to 1788

constitution: the basic laws by which a country or state is governed

document: a formal piece of writing

federal: having to do with the national government

guarantee: to make a promise

jury: a group of people chosen to decide the outcome of a court case

militia: a group of citizens who organize like soldiers in order to protect themselves

protect: to keep safe

protest: to strongly oppose something

ratify: to formally agree to something

representative: one who stands for a group of people

warrant: a document issued by a legal or government official giving law enforcement permission to take action to carry out the law

FOR MORE INFORMATION

Books

Leavitt, Amie Jane. *The Bill of Rights in Translation: What It Really Means*. North Mankato, MN: Capstone Press, 2018.

Mara, Wil. *Citizens' Rights*. Ann Arbor, MI: Cherry Lake Publishing, 2017.

Website

The Bill of Rights for Kids
kids.laws.com/bill-of-rights
Read about the Bill of Rights in detail here.

Publisher's note to educators and parents: Our editors have carefully reviewed this website to ensure that they are suitable for students. Many websites change frequently, however, and we cannot guarantee that a site's future contents will continue to meet our high standards of quality and educational value. Be advised that students should be closely supervised whenever they access the internet.

INDEX